"If you believe that people have no history worth mentioning, it's easy to believe they have no humanity worth defending."

— William Loren Katz

Abandoned History Series

This book is part of the Abandoned History Series published by the Museum of disABILITY History, People Inc., and People Ink Press.

Due to a general reluctance to discuss the way those in need were treated in the past, records and memories of the institutions that served the poor, sick, and disabled are fading—into a world of abandoned history.

The Museum of disABILITY History is committed to preserving the important historical record of these almost-forgotten institutions.

This book is a part of that effort.

On the Edge of Town:
Almshouses of Western New York

Lynn S. Beman and Elizabeth A. Marotta

With contributions by:
Reid V. Dunlavey and Douglas A. Platt

> Editor's Note: The exact language of the historical periods researched for this book is retained for historical accuracy. No offense is intended toward any individual or group.

This book, originally printed in 2006, has been updated with additional historical information and period maps that show the locations of the facilities.

Copyright © 2011, Museum of disABILITY History

All rights reserved. No part of this publication may be reproduced, stored in a retrieval system, or transmitted in any form by any process—electronic, mechanical, photocopying, recording, or otherwise—without the prior written permission of the copyright owner and the Museum of disABILITY History. For reprint permission information, please contact the Museum of disABILITY History at 716.629.3626.

Design by Rachel Gottorff, People Inc.

Publisher: James M. Boles, EdD

ISBN 13: 978-0-9845983-2-8
ISBN 10: 0-9845983-2-4

People Ink Press
in association with the
Museum of disABILITY History
3826 Main Street
Buffalo, New York 14226

PEOPLE INK PRESS

Dedication

To the memory of the men, women, and children who lived, worked, and sometimes died in the almshouses of Western New York.

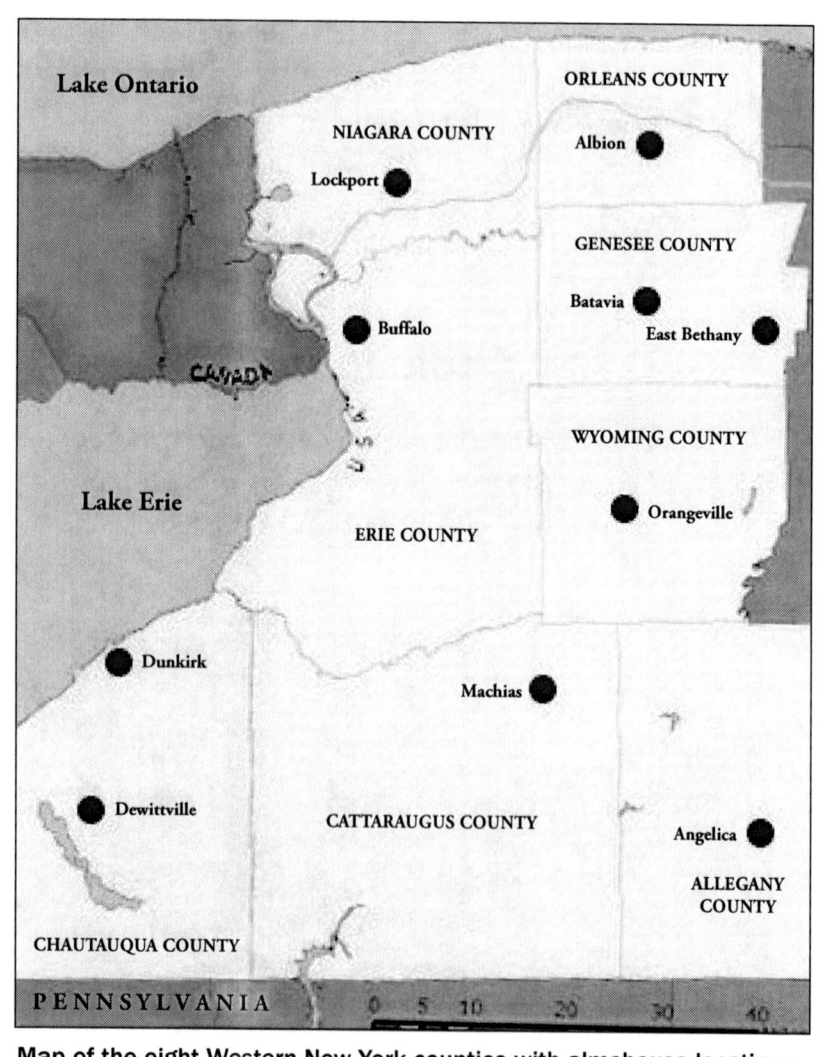

Map of the eight Western New York counties with almshouse locations.

Table of Contents

Map of Western New York Almshouses...................Inside Cover

Introduction 1

Allegany County Home.. 7

Cattaraugus County Almshouse and Insane Asylum................ 13

Chautauqua County Home... 21

Erie County Poorhouse, Home and Infirmary......................... 29

Genesee County Home and Insane Asylum............................ 39

Niagara County Almshouse 47

Orleans County Almshouse... 57

Wyoming County Poorhouse... 69

Bibliography... 77

Acknowledgments... 83

Index... 85

Images from the Museum of disABILITY History files, Buffalo, New York.
Dorothea Dix, top; poorhouse idiot, bottom left; poorhouse imbecile, bottom right, c. 1886.

Introduction

> *What is an almshouse? One would naturally suppose it to be the last refuge of the old - men and women too weak to work, alone in the world, homeless, friendless, penniless... It is the last refuge of the old; it is the winter hotel of the vagrant; it is the pest-house for the sick; the asylum for the feeble-minded. It is where they commit the dependent, the paupers, the defective and the delinquent.*
>
> — "He's only a Pauper, Whom Nobody Owns!" by James Oppenheim, *The American Magazine*, June 1910

People who were unable to care for themselves because of mental illness, or intellectual or physical disabilities, were for centuries included with people called paupers or "the poor." As recently as the twentieth century, lists of paupers residing in almshouses included people who were identified as "feeble-minded, insane, deaf and dumb, blind, delinquent, defective, promiscuous, or indigent."

New York State has always been among the leaders in providing care for people who were unable to care for themselves. In 1652, in what was New Netherland, residents of the Dutch village of Beverwijck (now the city of Albany) built an almshouse that was operated by the deacons of the Dutch Reformed Church. This almshouse was built on land provided by the government but its relief operations were funded by contributions made by Beverwijck residents. It was the first publicly funded institution in North America to care for the poor and disabled, preceding an almshouse built on Manhattan Island in 1658 and a poorhouse in Boston in 1684.

In Massachusetts Colony, the poor laws of 1693 included an "Act for the Relief of Ideotts and Distracted Persons," which required all communities in the colony to provide care for "ideotts and distracted persons when no relations appear to undertake the care of them..."

Initially, help for the poor was provided through "outdoor relief," a system used by towns throughout the colonies. Individuals unable to care for themselves and who had no relatives to provide care would be housed with local families.

Under this system, also known as the "New England System," paupers were "bound out" to contractors (actually local townspeople or farmers) who were paid by the community to care for them. Sometimes contractors were chosen by a kind of reverse auction: the one who bid the least amount of money was awarded the care of the pauper. Although paupers were not supposed to perform manual labor for the contractor, this was often not the case in an era when nearly everyone had to work hard to survive.

As populations increased, so did the number of people who needed assistance. Communities began to serve the poor through "indoor relief" in the form of almshouses. By the early nineteenth century, many communities in the United States began to build almshouses, also called poorhouses, to provide care for adults and children who were unable to care for themselves.

In 1824, New York State established a county almshouse law requiring each county in the state to build an almshouse to care for the poor, which included many people with mental or physical disabilities. New York State was among the first to require counties to provide such care. People with disabilities were then distinguished by two classes: those able to work or those unable to work.

Often the almshouse included a farm that was worked by the residents, allowing the almshouse a measure of self-sufficiency. Sometimes a county would later build an insane asylum or hospital as part of the almshouse complex.

Children with mental retardation or developmental disabilities (those considered to be "idiots, feeble-minded, or crippled") were frequently sent to an almshouse when their parents were unable or unwilling to care for them. Such children were sometimes abandoned by their parents, and the community would place them in the almshouse to be cared for and perhaps even educated.

Almshouses were established to serve as "good places," somewhere for people to go to when they were in need of food, clothing, shelter, or rudimentary medical care. For example, a laborer or farmer who was injured or seriously ill might be cared for in the almshouse until he was well enough to work. A widow unable to support herself and her young children or the aged infirm without family or persons with disabilities might all go to the poorhouse for care where they would reside for a few weeks or months, or even for the remainder of their lives.

Unfortunately—despite the best of intentions—conditions at some poorhouses became deplorable, even by the standards of the early nineteenth century. Official government inspection reports of some almshouses described overcrowding, disease and epidemics, malnourishment, and sometimes cruelty or physical abuse.

In the mid 1800s, Dorothea Dix began visiting jails, asylums, and poorhouses in the United States. In 1848, she lobbied Congress and state governments for better care of residents. In particular, she demanded that the "insane" and the "feebleminded" be treated more humanely and placed into more suitable places for appropriate treatment. She further demanded that they be separated from the truly poor and from criminal populations. Dix worked hard to ensure better care for people with disabilities, paving the way for larger, specialized public institutions.

In Syracuse, New York, the State Asylum for Idiots opened in 1855. Many almshouses in New York State transferred their "idiotic and feeble-minded children" to the new asylum, although only children ages six to sixteen received training. The transfer was one of the first examples of children and people with disabilities, who were once considered paupers, being properly channeled in a humanitarian way toward institutions of care more tailored to their specific needs.

The names of facilities changed over time, and often each county used multiple names for the same county complex. "Poorhouse" was an earlier term, and "almshouse" the more common term, but you will also see "county farm," "county home," "county asylum," and "county infirmary."

Under their new names and sometimes in different locations, county homes and infirmaries were able to focus on housing the elderly and infirm who were financially unable to support themselves.

Because of deteriorating conditions or a need for greater capacity, many counties relocated their almshouses several times. County almshouses operating for many years and considered primary county almshouses by local historians are the main focus of each chapter. Multiple locations are noted.

Editor's note: The exact language of the historical periods researched for this book is retained for historical accuracy. No offense is intended toward any individual or group.

OVER THE HILL TO THE POOR-HOUSE
Over the hill to the poor-house I'm trudgin' my weary way -
I am a woman of seventy, and only a trifle gray -
I, who am smart an' chipper, for all the years I've told,
As many another woman that's only half as old.

O'er the hill to the poor-house - I can't quite make it clear!
Over the hill to the poor-house - it seems so horrid queer!
Many a step I've taken a-toilin' to and fro,
But this is a sort of journey I never thought to go.

What is the use of heapin' on me a pauper's shame?
Am I lazy or crazy? Am I blind or lame?
True, I am not so supple, nor yet so awful stout.
But charity ain't no favor, if one can live without.
By Will Carleton, 1868

Buildings at the Allegany County Home, late 1800s.

Photos in this section courtesy of Craig Braack, Allegany County historian.

Allegany County Home
1831-1960s
Angelica, New York

Allegany County, organized in 1806, is located in the Southern Tier of New York State on the Pennsylvania border. It is comprised of a portion of the forest-covered Allegany Mountains, with rich farmland in the north and beautiful scenery. The Genesee River cuts the county in half as it flows northward toward Lake Ontario. Its western section was part of the Holland Land Purchase, while the eastern portions were part of the Morris Reserve. The first commercial oil wells in the United States were drilled near the Allegany Town of Wellsville.

The Allegany County Home, sometimes also called the Allegany County Poorhouse, was constructed in 1831 in the picturesque village of Angelica, which was once the county seat. The poorhouse served as a haven for the "unfortunates of the county," those incapable of caring for themselves for reasons that included poverty, old age, and disability.

Allegany County Home: "County Alms House," 1869.

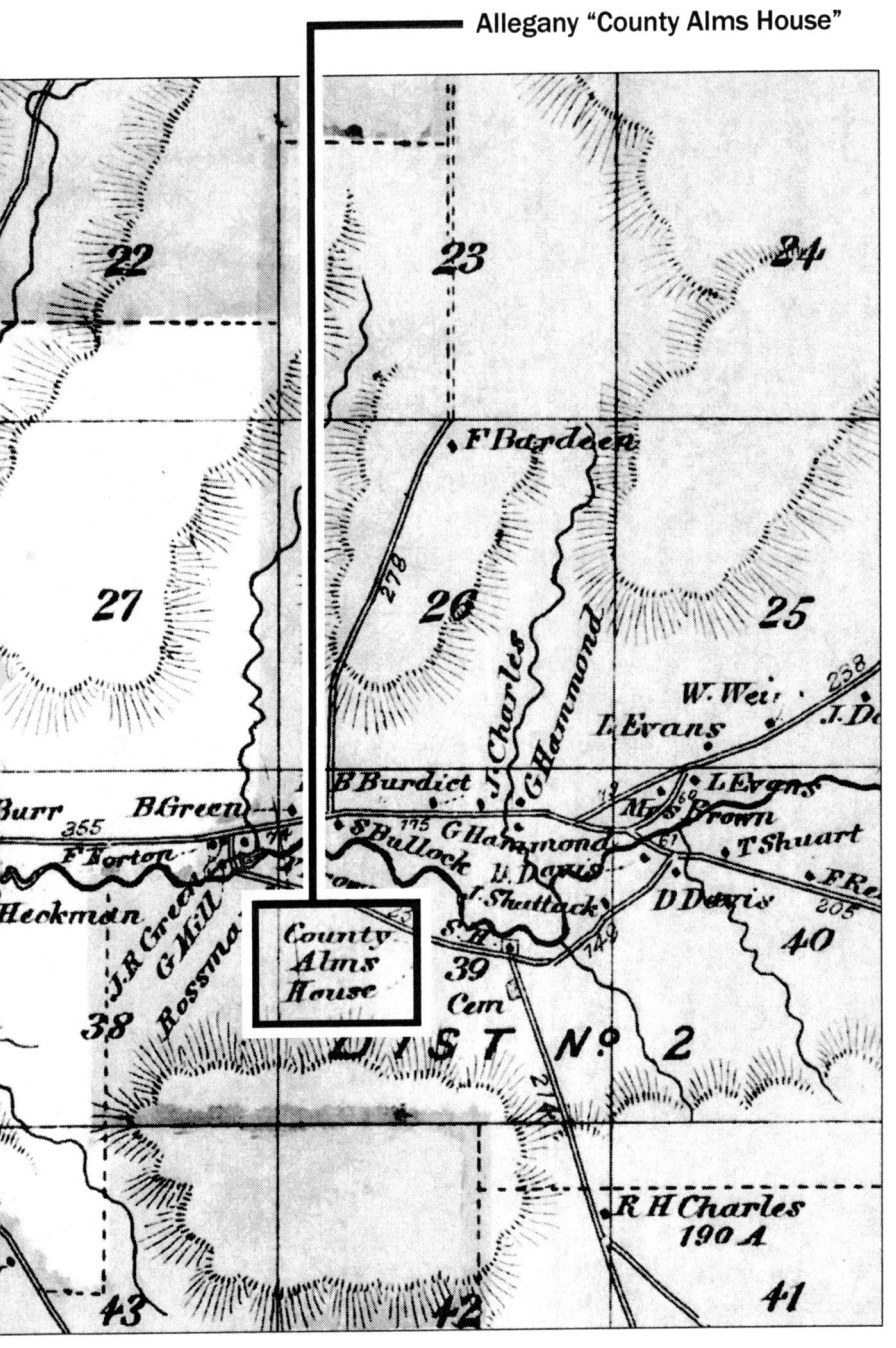

Angelica, Allegany County, 1869.
Map by D. G. Beers and Company.

10   On the Edge of Town: *Almshouses of Western New York*

Living quarters at the Allegany County Home, late 1800s.

An official inspection of the Allegany County Home in 1857 reported that the residents included six people who were "lunatics" and "idiots."

An article written in 1880 by the editor of the *Friendship Chronicle* noted:

> The inmates appear to be well supplied with good wholesome food and some indeed are treated to luxuries scarcely to be looked for in their condition. Indeed Mr. and Mrs. Weaver [the keepers of the poorhouse] evidently do the very best they can, with what the County affords, to render the condition of the "unfortunates" as endurable as possible.

In 1923, fire destroyed nearly the entire structure of the Allegany County Home. Fire crews were unable to extinguish the flames because a well located near the boiler room where the fire began was destroyed before the firemen arrived. The only building to escape ruin was the men's dormitory. Casualties of the fire included seven elderly, bed-ridden women, a male patient, and three employees.

Following the fire, the Allegany County Home was rebuilt and remained in operation until 1960. Today, the property and buildings are owned by a farmer who rents out the original caretaker's home.

As was the case at many other poorhouses or county homes across New York State, a nearby cemetery was used to inter the bodies of residents who died while in the county's care.

In Angelica, the "Until the Day Dawn" cemetery was the first of two cemeteries used by Allegany County. Each grave was marked by a simple headstone without a name or date, only a number protecting the anonymity of the deceased. Names of the deceased and corresponding grave numbers were recorded in the Angelica Cemetery Register, the only means of linking the name of the deceased (from 1831–1923) to the graves. Tragically, the early register was destroyed in the 1923 fire. (New York State Archives has almshouse records for all counties of New York.)

The old Stone House of the Cattaraugus County Almshouse and Insane Asylum, 1890s.

Photos in this section courtesy of Carol Ruth, Cattaraugus County Historian's Office.

Cattaraugus County Almshouse and Insane Asylum
1835-1960
Machias, New York

Cattaraugus County is located in the southwestern portion of Western New York, bordering Pennsylvania. The county's name originated from a Seneca Indian word meaning "bad smelling banks," due to the natural gas that seeped from the rock formations along Cattaraugus Creek. In 1808, Cattaraugus County was formed from Genesee County, although the county government was not organized until 1817.

The Cattaraugus County Almshouse and Insane Asylum, established in 1833 in the rural community of Machias, was later called the Cattaraugus County Home and Infirmary or the County Farm and Infirmary. The almshouse and farm buildings suffered a fire in 1846, but the buildings were rebuilt. One of the major buildings of the home is the Stone House, built in 1868, and the last remaining structure of the almshouse. It is a source of historic pride for county residents. According to the Cattaraugus County Historical Society, there were sixty residents of the Stone

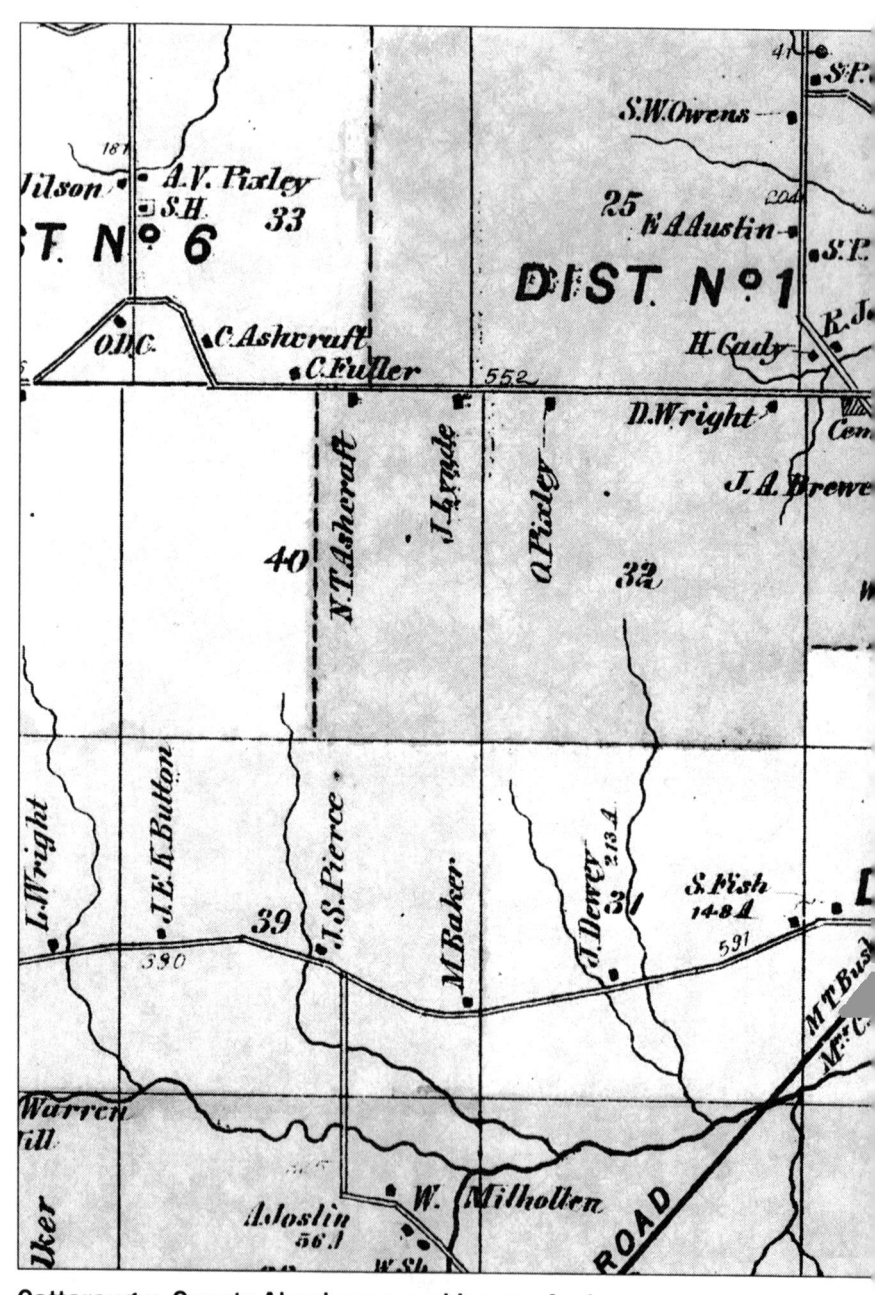

Cattaraugus County Almshouse and Insane Asylum: "Cattaraugus Alms House," 1869.

Cattaraugus County
Map by D. G. Beers and Company, 1879.

House by 1885, including "paupers, idiots, and epileptics."

The almshouse included the county insane asylum which housed individuals considered to be mentally ill. An 1857 report by the Committee on Charitable Institutions notes that:

> *In the house is one idiot and one blind person. Intemperance is the cause of one half the pauperism here. The house is a poor one and the poor, especially the insane, are illy [sic] cared for...the insane sleep on straw, with very little clothing, the straw becoming filled with filth before being changed. Two are confined in these cells. The insane are attended by a male pauper.*

Front view of the kitchen and dining room, Cattaraugus County Almshouse and Insane Asylum, early 1900s.

Cattaraugus County Almshouse and Insane Asylum   17

Image from an old postcard titled "For God's Poor" (large rear building) and "For the Insane" (buildings on right), Cattaraugus County Almshouse and Insane Asylum.

Winter view of the Cattaraugus County Almshouse and Insane Asylum, 1920s.

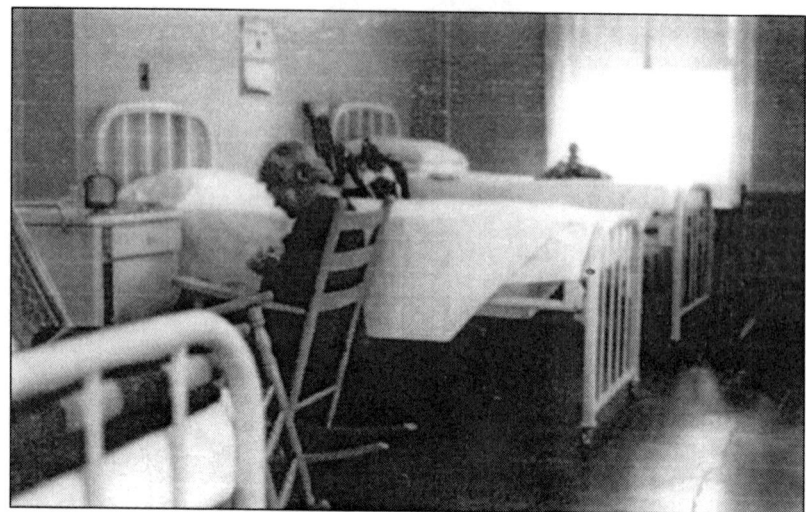

An elderly woman passing time in her quarters at the Cattaraugus County Almshouse and Insane Asylum, early 1920s.

Residents of the Cattaraugus County Almshouse and Insane Asylum, 1920s.

Cattaraugus County Almshouse attempted to be a self-sufficient community. Crops raised on the almshouse farm included buckwheat, oats, feed corn for livestock, cabbage, potatoes, beets, turnips, carrots, onions, sweet corn, peas, tomatoes, apples, parsnips, salsify (similar to parsnips), and lettuce. Most of the food and dairy products consumed by the residents came from crops and animals raised on the premises. Although most of the buildings that once stood on the grounds of the Cattaraugus County Almshouse and Insane Asylum have long been demolished, the Stone House still stands and carries on the tradition of care for people in the county. Today, the Stone House is home to six county departments including the Historian's Office and Research Library, a museum, a satellite office of the County Health Department, Community Service and Probation, and the Council on Alcohol and Substance Abuse.

20　On the Edge of Town: *Almshouses of Western New York*

Main building at the Chautauqua County Almshouse and Asylum, early 1900s.

Photo in this section courtesy of Jack Ericson.

Chautauqua County Home
1832-1962
Dewittville, New York

Chautauqua County is located in the southwestern corner of New York State, bordered on two sides by Pennsylvania and Lake Erie. Along its Lake Erie shoreline are some of the finest Concord grape vineyards in the world. The county is also noted for Chautauqua Lake, a popular summer resort area, and the internationally renowned Chautauqua Institution.

In 1832, the original Chautauqua County Almshouse and Asylum was erected on ninety acres of land a few miles southeast of the Village of Mayville in Dewittville, a small community located on the northern shore of Chautauqua Lake. A second building was constructed in 1850 to house the insane, but was replaced in 1867 with a larger, three-story structure.

The county tried to provide proper care to the residents of the poorhouse and insane asylum. According to a nineteenth century document provided by the Chautauqua County Historical Society:

Chautauqua County Home: "County Farm Aslylum" and "Alms House," 1881.

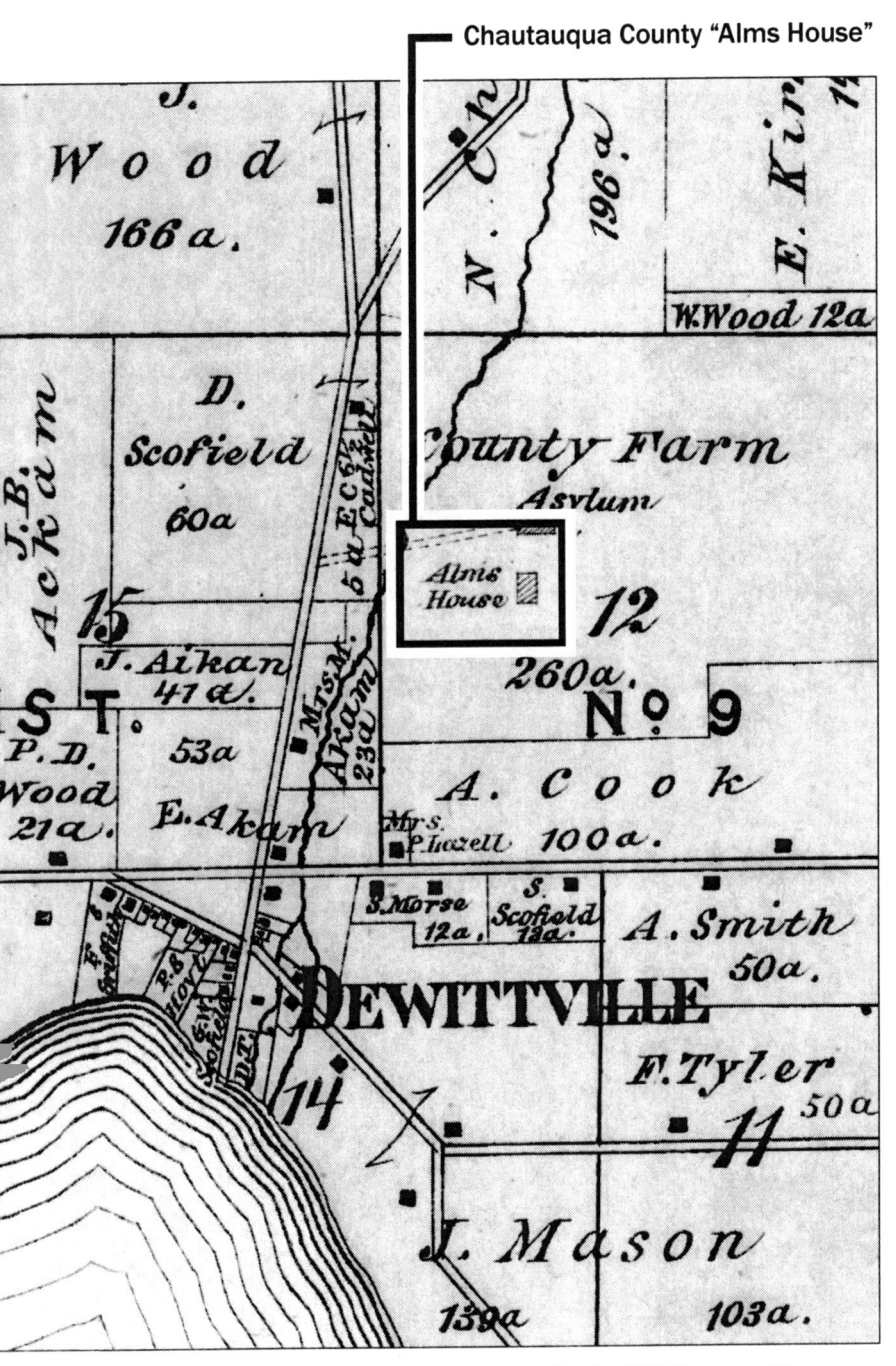

Map by F. W. Beers and Company

Residents shucking peas at the Chautauqua County Almshouse and Asylum, early 1900s.

> *The sick and infirm, males and females, and those who have families and those who have not, idiots, lunatics and maniacs are all classed, and kept in different and suitable apartments.*

Additionally, a doctor visited the residents daily and also made special visits to the home when needed. In 1869 the county paid him an annual salary of $225.

From its beginnings, the county intended that the almshouse and poor farm be self-sustaining. Residents who were capable of working, did so. Women residents baked, sewed, spun, and did the laundry and other domestic tasks. Men worked the farm itself, raising crops and tending livestock. While the poor farm did not provide an economic base for the county, it defrayed much of the cost of its own operation. The "1891 Report on the Poorhouses in the Eighth Judicial District" noted:

> The Chautauqua County poor-house has long been noted for its excellent industrial system... Although the kinds of occupation have changed with the changed character of the inmates, there now being fewer skilled in mechanic arts, its well-earned reputation for industry is sustained.

In 1851, the New York and Erie Railroad was completed from New York City's harbor to Dunkirk, linking the Great Lakes to the Atlantic Ocean. Soon, a growing number of immigrants began arriving in Dunkirk by train. With nowhere to go and no means of support, these immigrant paupers were transported to the county poor farm.

By the 1860s, Chautauqua County was submitting more claims than most other counties to the State Commissioners of Emigration, seeking reimbursement for "the care of these emigrant paupers." In order to get reimbursed by the state, the county poor farm maintained separate ledgers documenting the aid provided to emigrants. The ledgers provide a great deal of information about those who received relief, including names, ages, nationalities, dates of arrival, and carrier (ship). The superintendent of the poor also recorded deaths that occurred at the farm. An example from one of the ledgers illustrates that the superintendent's opinion frequently made its way into the entries:

> Augustus W. was admitted age 64 in Oct 1864... INTEMPERATE. This man has the appearance of being a raw Irishman though he denies it. I verily

Back view of the Chautauqua County Almshouse and Asylum, early 1900s.

> *believe him to be an Irishman-he is very untruthful and unreliable...James O'B. [also Irish]...Said to be insane from study for the priesthood.*

In the twentieth century, the name of the county almshouse and poor farm was changed to the Chautauqua County Home and Infirmary.

During a genealogical study of the residents at the county home conducted by the Chautauqua County Historical Society, information about a world-famous film and television star was discovered:

> *The name Wm Orcutt...appeared and reappeared in admissions to the county house. That Wm. was indeed Lucy's great-grandfather...a pregnant 23 year old Mrs. Helen Orcutt showed up in the admission record with three children...[one of the children] Flora Belle Orcutt grew up and married Frederick Hunt and was the mother of Deseree Evelyn Hunt, Lucille Ball's mother...Lucie Arnez Luckinbill loves the story...when her parents were alive, she asked no questions about family history, and had never visited her mother's home town. When she did come to Jamestown for the first annual "Lucy Fest," she so enjoyed listening to the reminiscences of all who remembered her mother's girlhood.*

In 1961, the county home and infirmary were relocated to a modern facility in Dunkirk. No buildings from the Dewittville site remain, but the poor farm cemetery is still owned and maintained by Chautauqua County. The one-acre cemetery was first used in 1833 and by 1864 contained more than 600 burials. By the mid 1920s, use of the cemetery was discontinued; more than 1,600 individuals are believed to be buried there.

28 On the Edge of Town: *Almshouses of Western New York*

The Insane Asylum at the Erie County Almshouse, 1900.

Images in this section courtesy of Buffalo and Erie County Historical Society Research Library and the Museum of disABILITY History.

Erie County Poorhouse, Home and Infirmary 1829–1926 Buffalo, New York

Erie County is the largest and most populated county in Western New York. The county's western border is formed by Lake Erie and the Niagara River. Tonawanda Creek, which includes portions of the original Erie Canal, forms the northern border. Buffalo, the county's largest city, was laid out in 1800 by Joseph Ellicott, the head surveyor for the Holland Land Company. Erie County and Buffalo prospered with the opening of the Erie Canal in 1825. As a terminus for the Erie Canal, Buffalo rapidly became the "Gateway to the West" and at one time was the second busiest port in the United States.

In 1829, the county selected a site near Porter and Fargo Avenues, in what was then the Village of Black Rock, as the site to house its poor and indigent citizens. By 1850, the building was considered dilapidated and insufficient for those who were in need of care.

A new almshouse and poor farm were erected in 1850 on a 150-acre site on Main Street. The buildings were constructed of

Erie County Poorhouse: "County Poor House," 1866.

Erie "County Poor House"

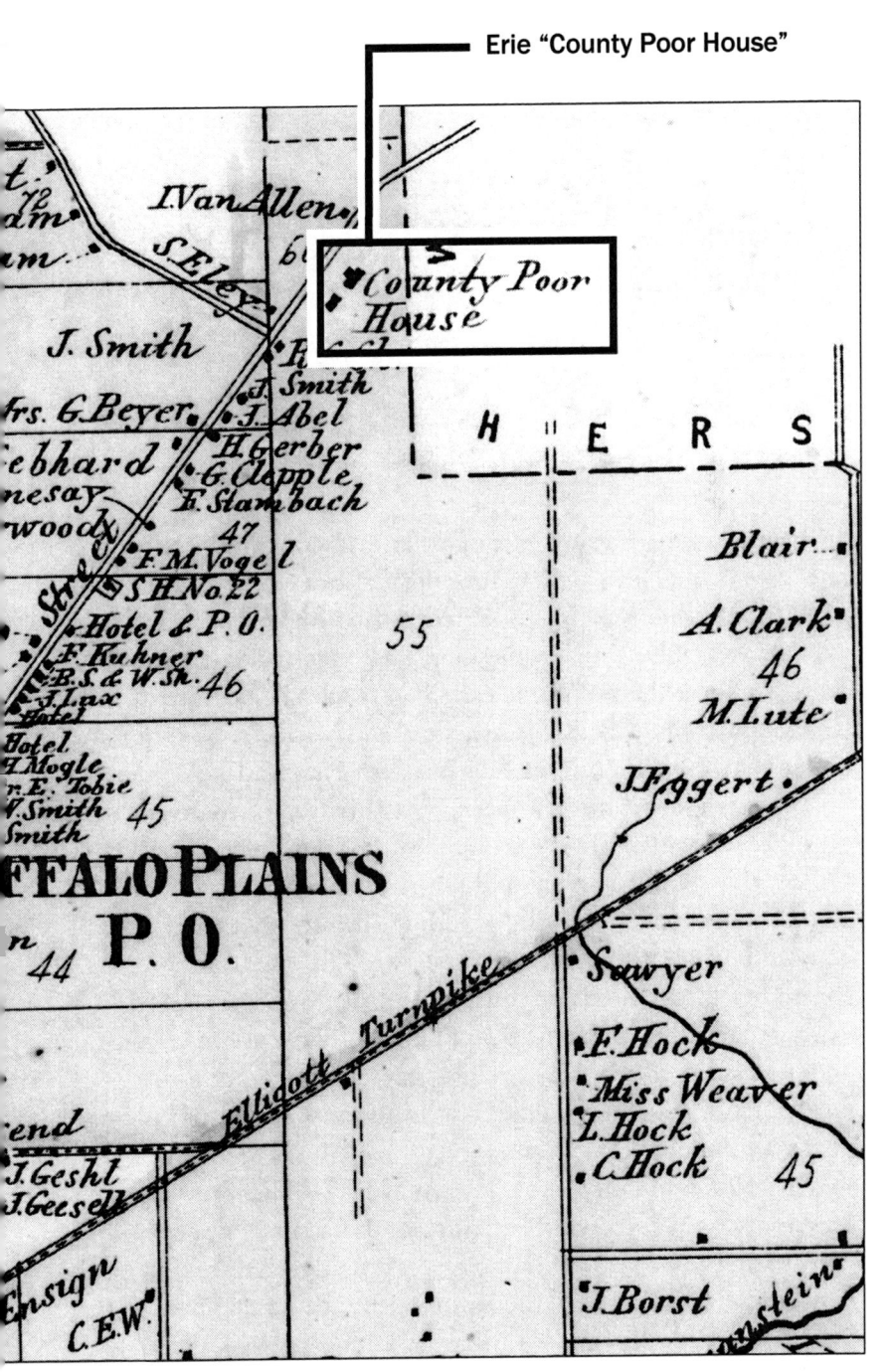

Map by Stone and Stewart

The New Erie County Almshouse, late 1800s.

limestone quarried from a farm farther east along Main Street. Fire, always a major problem for poorhouses at this time, didn't spare the almshouse, which suffered its first fire in 1855. The structure was rebuilt that same year. The buildings experienced other fires over the years, but were always rebuilt. Because of the large population of Erie County, almshouse facilities housed more citizens than other almshouses in Western New York.

Throughout its history, many other buildings needed for the operation of the almshouse and poor farm were erected on the property. A county hospital and maternity hospital served all county residents. Those with infectious diseases were accommodated in the "pest house" to keep disease from spreading. Tuberculosis, or consumption as it was then called, was rampant during the nineteenth and early twentieth centuries, and infected residents were housed in a separate ward of the facility. Children and the elderly were also separated from the rest of the almshouse population.

In 1874, a building (now known as Hayes Hall on the State University of New York at Buffalo's South Campus) was constructed to house the Insane Department of the Erie County Almshouse. At this point, the entire facility became known as the Erie County Almshouse and Insane Asylum. In 1893, the residents at the asylum were moved to the Buffalo State Hospital (known today as the Buffalo Psychiatric Center) as part of a statewide movement to provide specific care for those with mental illness. By 1894, the original insane asylum building had been converted to a 400-bed county hospital.

In 1906, almshouse nurses were given a separate building to reside in. Many of the county's citizens opposed the construction of the building and referred to it as the "nurses' mansion." Much of the dissention for the new complex can be attributed to the large sum of money the county spent to build it: approximately $60,000 for the building and $3,000 more for a tunnel for the nurses to walk between their quarters and the main complex.

Discussions regarding the separation of the almshouse and the county hospital remained a hot topic during the late nineteenth and early twentieth centuries. Although there was a move to separate the two for political reasons, the core issue was the stigmatization of people associated with the county hospital because it was considered part of the almshouse. The keeper of the almshouse was also the supervisor of the county hospital,

The Erie County Almshouse and Insane Asylum maternity ward building, now Wende Hall, early 1900s.

adding to the stigmatization associated with the hospital.

When University at Buffalo officials learned in 1907 that Erie County planned to relocate the almshouse, they decided that the almshouse grounds would be the perfect location for the development of its campus. The university, founded in 1846, needed more space to serve the growing number of students, and officials wanted to build a new, unified campus. In 1909, the university purchased 109 acres of land between Main Street and Bailey Avenue and later acquired an additional 72 acres from the county and private individuals. The land included the almshouse buildings and surrounding farm. The university hired notable architects, including E. B. Green, to redesign and renovate the existing almshouse buildings (such as Hayes Hall) and to design and construct new buildings.

Between the years of 1909 and 1926, although the university owned the grounds and facilities, the majority of the buildings

The nurses' building at the Erie County Almshouse and Insane Asylum, early 1900s.

Putting out a fire at the Erie County Almshouse and Insane Asylum, c. 1920s.

Residents evacuated during a fire at the Erie County Almshouse and Insane Asylum, 1920s.

The nursery at the Erie County Almshouse and Insane Asylum, early 1900s.

The apothecary at the Erie County Almshouse and Insane Asylum, early 1900s.

remained occupied by the "paupers." It was not until 1926 that renovations to the new university campus were complete and the last of the almshouse residents transferred to the new Erie County Home and Infirmary on Walden Avenue in Alden.

Today, some of the old county almshouse, poor farm, and hospital buildings still remain on the State University of New York at Buffalo's South Campus. Hayes Hall, which was the original county insane asylum and later the county hospital, now serves the School of Architecture and Planning. Crosby Hall stands on the site of the original almshouse building. Wende Hall, once the county maternity hospital, houses classrooms and offices. Also still standing on the campus is a single story building left over from the almshouse days, now known as Hayes D., and another old building named Townsend Hall, the former almshouse nurse's building.

The Erie County Home and Infirmary is still in operation in Alden. Funded by the county, and in association with the Erie County Medical Center, services are mainly provided to elderly persons in need of care. The Erie County Medical Center, formerly stigmatized because of pauperism, is now considered one of the best health care facilities in the state and has the largest trauma and cardiovascular treatment centers in Western New York.

Birds-eye view of the Genesee County Poorhouse.

Photos in this section courtesy of Susan Conklin, Genesee County historian.

Genesee County Home and Insane Asylum
1827-1974
East Bethany, New York

Genesee County, organized in 1802 and once part of Ontario County, originally encompassed all of Western New York. Seven subsequent counties were formed from Genesee County. The word "Genesee" is a Seneca Indian word meaning "beautiful valley," and undoubtedly reflects the magnificent Genesee River gorge and surrounding land. The county seat has always been located in Batavia, where the Holland Land Company Office was located and where the first settlers began purchasing land as early as November of 1800.

The Genesee County Poorhouse, later known as the Genesee County Home and Insane Asylum, was in the rural town of East Bethany. In 1827, the poorhouse, earlier used as a stagecoach tavern, was located in a brick building near the corner of Bethany Center and Raymond Roads. This site was selected because it represented the geographical center of Genesee County (which also included what is now Wyoming County).

The Genesee County Home and Asylum sent the children

Genesee County Home: "County Poor House," 1866.

Genesee "County Poor House"

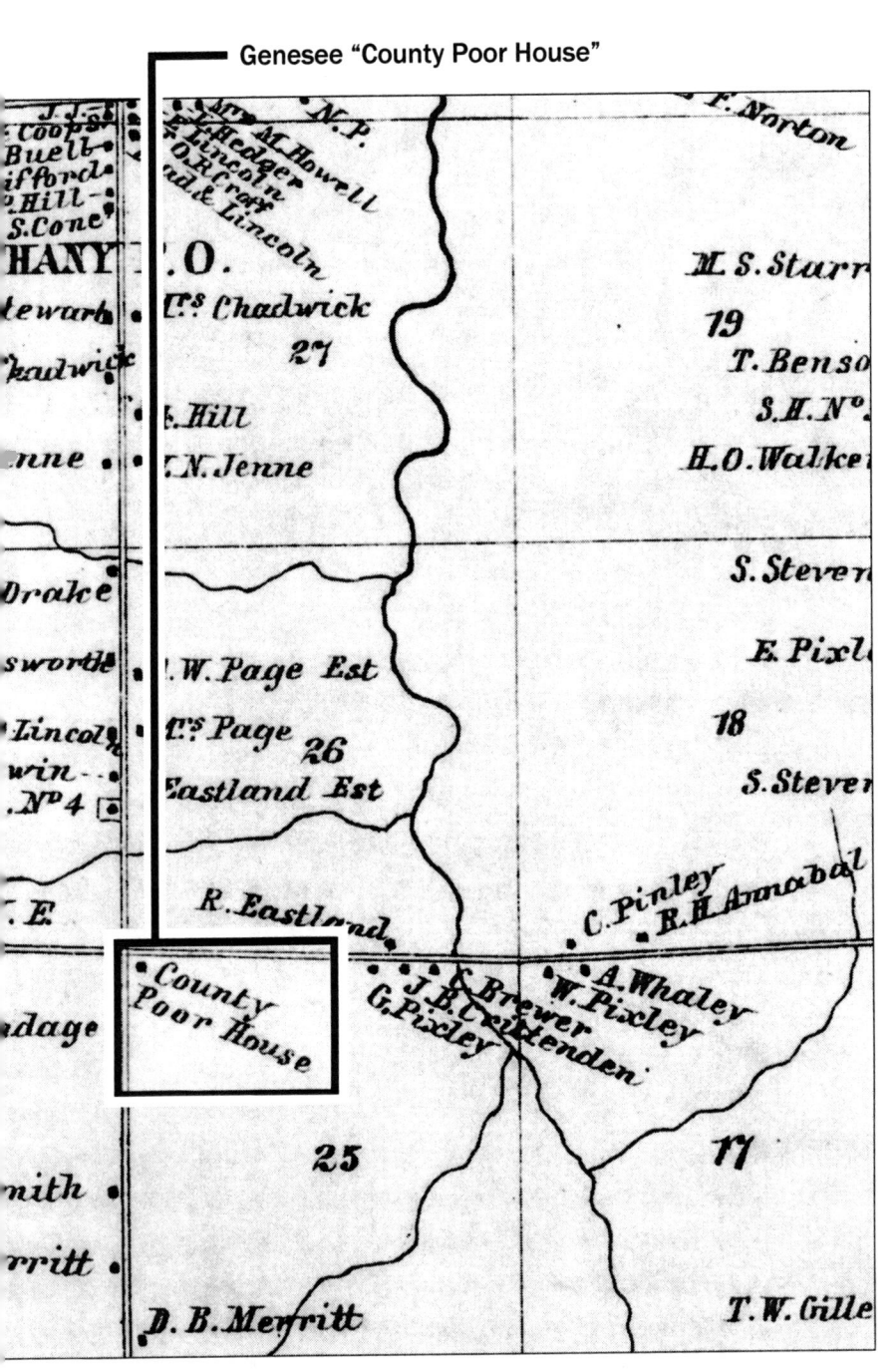

Map by Stone and Stewart

The Genesee County Poorhouse today, now Rolling Hills Country Mall.

Workers at the Genesee County Poorhouse, early 1900s.

who resided in the county facility to neighboring schools to be educated. The first schoolhouse in the county was built in 1801 in LeRoy. Ingham University, also located in LeRoy, opened in 1857. Ingham was the first university exclusively for women in the United States. In 1865, Batavia became the home for the New York State School for the Blind, an institution still open today and continuing to provide educational services to people with visual impairments.

As was often the case in other counties, children were admitted to the poorhouse because they were orphans, abandoned by their parents because of a disability, or because their parents were ill, disabled, or financially unable to care for them. Sometimes babies or toddlers were abandoned because they were born out of wedlock. Children who became dependent upon local government for care might, in the nineteenth and twentieth centuries, have been "bound out" to local families or farmers who were often seeking cheap labor. Others, especially those who were unable to perform manual labor because of physical or mental impairments, would remain in the poorhouses or orphanages.

In 1828, a young girl considered to be an "idiot" entered the Genesee County Poorhouse when she was nine years old and remained there until her death. An indication of how society viewed such children is seen in the following newspaper account that was intended to serve as her obituary:

> *For 58 years she has been an inmate, never having spent a single night away from that institution...her personal habits were filthy beyond all description, which made her a great care and burden...Her cost to the county during the 58 years [was] $7000, and this amount would not begin to pay for the trouble she has made if an attendant had been hired to care for*

> her. Why such persons are permitted to be a burden for so many years, while scores of beautiful lives come to an early end, is one of the mysteries that will not be solved in this life.
>
> —*Progressive Batavian*, January 29, 1886

Residents of the poorhouse (adults and children) were often punished for misdeeds and bad behavior. Solitary confinement was one of the more common forms of punishment in almshouses. A document obtained from the Genesee County Historian's Office, related to the bylaws of the poorhouse, discusses this form of punishment:

> The keeper of the poor…may at his discretion, confine any pauper in a solitary cell for ill conduct, but not for a longer time than 48 hours without the direction of at least one of the superintendants [sic]. In all cases of solitary confinement, the prisoner shall be debarred seeing or conversing with any person except the keeper or the persons employed by him…his food shall consist of bread and water only, and any person who shall have communication with such person or prisoner, without the consent of the keeper, shall be punished with a like confinement.

Genesee County closed the poorhouse in 1927 when the facility moved to Batavia. Today, one may still visit the remains of the Genesee County Home and Insane Asylum, which is owned and operated by a private citizen as the "Rolling Hills Country Mall." The building is allegedly haunted by those who resided and perished in the home. The Rolling Hills Mall offers a "ghost hunt" at which people visit or spend a night in the home in hopes of encountering such spirits.

Front view of the original Niagara County Poorhouse and farm on Gothic Hill, late 1800s.

Unless otherwise noted, all images in this section courtesy of the Museum of disABILITY History.

Niagara County Almshouse
1829–1979
Lockport, New York

Niagara County is one of the larger counties of Western New York and was formed from Genesee County in 1808. Both the American Falls and Bridal Veil Falls are within Niagara County. Niagara Falls has been known since the mid-nineteenth century as "the honeymoon capital of the world." "Niagara," from the Seneca word *onigara*, means "thunder of waters." Many Western New York counties derive their names from the Seneca language.

In accordance with the New York State Poorhouse Law of 1824, Niagara County incorporated a poorhouse five years later in 1829 on what is now Niagara Street Extension and Gothic Hill Road in Lockport, the first of two sites of the home. In 1829, ninety-one acres were appropriated for a poorhouse and poor farm and a modest frame building was constructed for the care of the residents. In 1833, a three-story limestone building was erected to "better accommodate the paupers of the county." In 1845, another addition was made to the stone house when two,

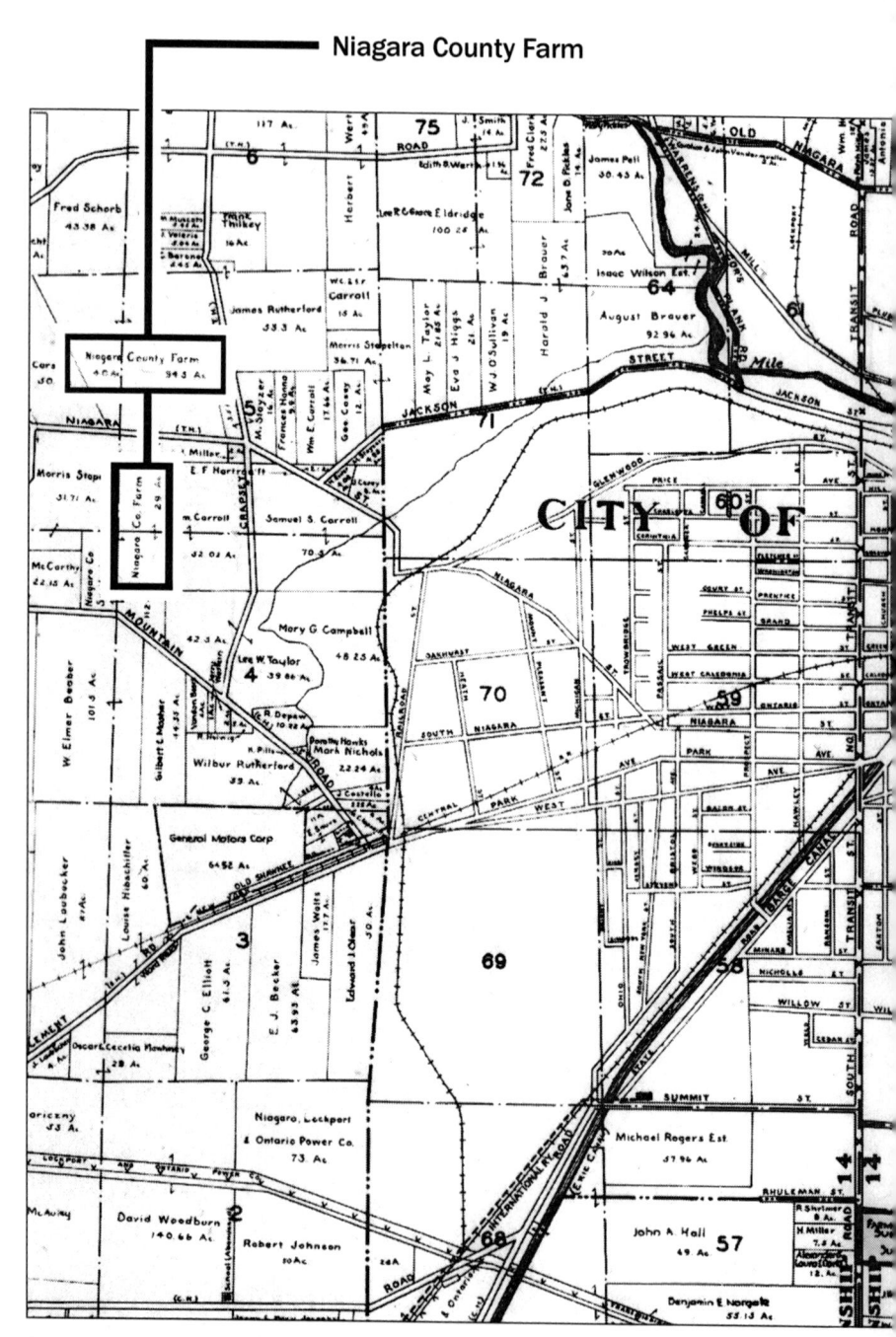

Locations of the old almshouse on Niagara Street Extension and the new almshouse (Niagara County Infirmary) on Davison Road.

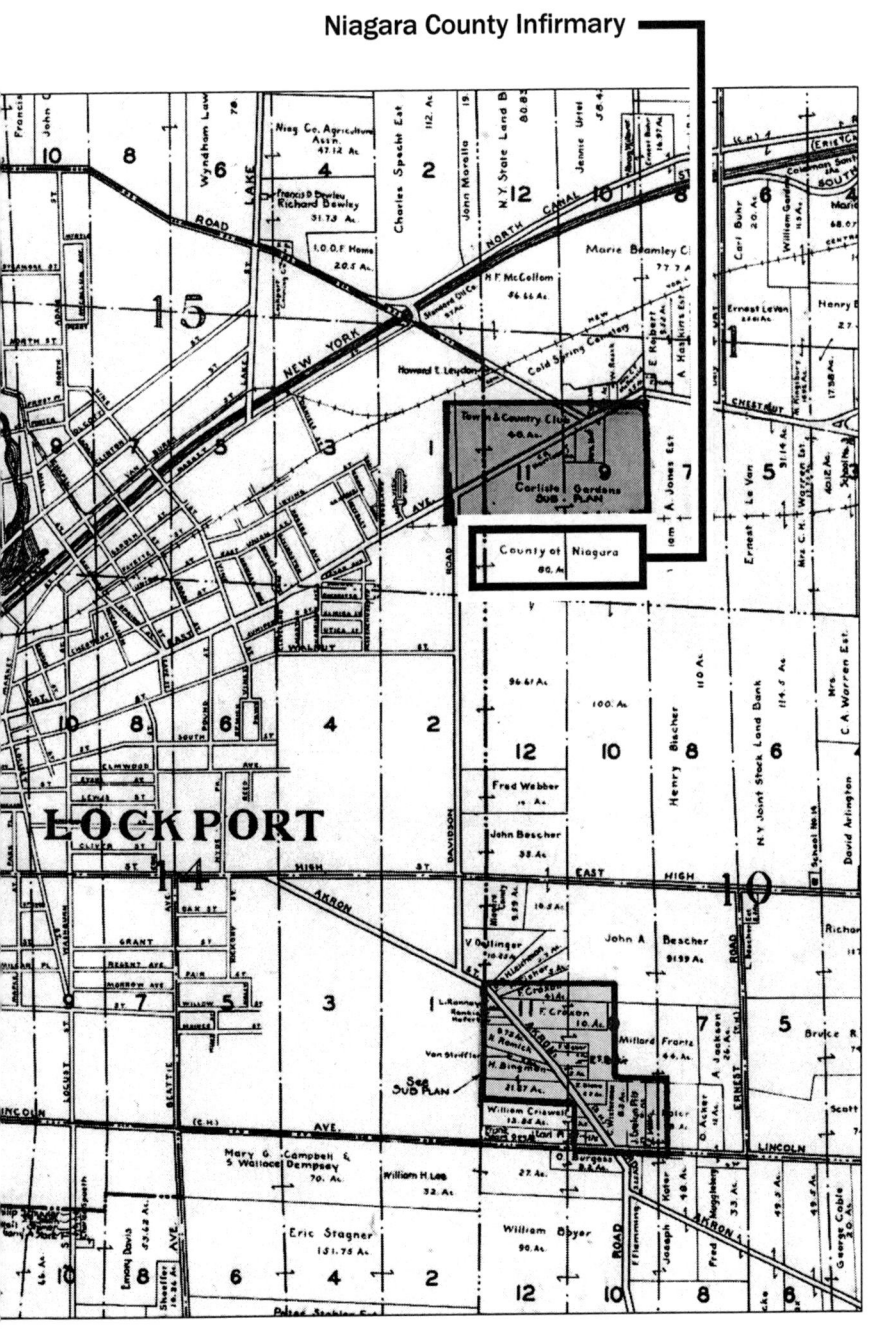

Niagara County, 1938, Town of Lockport.
Map by Niagara Frontier Planning Board.

The original Niagara County Poorhouse on Gothic Hill, late 1800s.

Front view of original Niagara County Poorhouse, Gothic Hill, early 1900s.

Original Niagara County Poorhouse, Gothic Hill, 1909.

three-story wings were built. The east wing was "entirely devoted to the care of the insane."

Although children in the Niagara County Poorhouse were schooled at the home, a law passed in 1875 required children living in the state's poorhouses to be relocated and provided with more specific care and education.

In Niagara County, many children who were between the ages of three and thirteen were moved in 1871 from the poorhouse to the Home for the Friendless, which was located on High Street in the City of Lockport. In 1892, this facility was relocated to an estate on Lake Road in the Town of Lockport and in 1917 renamed Wyndham Lawn Home for Children. The campus is still in use today, serving children and adolescents with mental health diagnoses.

The original stone poorhouse on Niagara Street remained in operation until the early 1900s. However, the state fire marshal declared this building a "fire trap," and despite repeated requests

Photo: Michelle Brant, 2010.
Home for the Friendless, 387 High Street, Lockport, New York. Children from the almshouse were relocated here.

by the fire marshal to either renovate the building or erect a new one, the home remained in operation. In 1912, the fire marshal gave an ultimatum: the county could either close the facility or begin work on a new building. If they did nothing, the county would be fined $50 per day for each day the fire marshal's demands were ignored.

The old almshouse property served Niagara County in three final roles. The hospital became the county's first tuberculosis hospital in 1915, in 1917 the buildings and property were used for the Niagara Industrial Prison Farm, and the County Jail was built on the grounds in 1960.

In 1915, the county broke ground for construction of the Niagara County Infirmary on Davison Road to replace the old poorhouse, and that same year, residents from the old stone building were transferred to the new site.

Among the many hundreds of people who lived in the

Niagara County Almshouse 53

Niagara County Infirmary campus on Davison Road, 1915. The new Niagara County Poorhouse.

Unless otherwise noted, photos in this section courtesy of Niagara County Historian's Office, Niagara County Historical Society, and Museum of disABILITY History.

Back view of New Niagara County Infirmary, Davison Road (1940s).

The new Niagara County Infirmary on Davison Road, 1915.

county poorhouse and infirmary was a dare-devil of international fame. Annie Edson Taylor, the first person to go over the Canadian/Horseshoe Falls in a barrel (October 24th, 1901), was an occupant of the Niagara County Infirmary. Despite her fame, Taylor was penniless at the time of her death. She died at the infirmary in Lockport in 1921 at 83 years old.

Today, a small memorial sits behind the Davison Road site dedicated to those, including children, who died in the poorhouse. Remnants of the old brick buildings that once comprised the Niagara County Infirmary are still visible on Davison Road.

Near the old poorhouse on Gothic Hill/Niagara Street Extension was a cemetery for its residents, but today only a few dozen graves are marked with small stones. Over 1400 people are said to be buried at the old poorhouse cemetery.

Main building at the Orleans County Poorhouse, early 1900s.

Unless otherwise noted, photos in this section courtesy of C. W. Lattin, Orleans County historian.

Orleans County Almshouse 1830-1960
Albion, New York

Orleans County, named for Andrew Jackson's 1814 victory in New Orleans, was established in 1824. Situated along the southern shore of Lake Ontario, Orleans County is notable for its rich deposits of red sandstone, often called Medina Sandstone, once used to build sidewalks in many cities, including Buffalo and New York City. The sandstone was used to build many of New York's famous "brownstone" townhouses. The renowned architect, Henry Hobson Richardson, utilized this natural resource in building the Richardson Complex at Buffalo State Hospital (now the Buffalo Psychiatric Center). Orleans County is still largely rural. Its rich farmland, known as "muck land," produces generous crops of produce such as cabbage and onions.

The Orleans County Almshouse, also referred to as the poorhouse or the county home, was built in 1830 in the Village of Albion on the southern bank of the Erie Canal. As did many counties, Orleans chose to locate its almshouse in the county seat.

Residents of the Orleans County Poorhouse, early 1900s.

Main building at the Orleans County Poorhouse, late 1890s.

Images of the dedication ceremony of the new Orleans County Poorhouse, early 1900s.

According to the first annual report of the New York State Board of Charities in 1868, the main building of the poorhouse was "built of brick three stories high." According to this same report, "...In the opinion of the keeper, who is also superintendent and has had charge of the Orleans county poorhouse for over eight years, the buildings are entirely unfitted for the use to which they are applied." At the time of this investigation, it was also noted that:

> *The building is much out of repair, the floors broken, and the plastering off in many places. It was stated that the authorities contemplate the erection of a new building during the coming year, which is much needed to meet in a suitable manner, the wants of the poor dependent upon the county for support.*

Orleans County "Alms Ho."

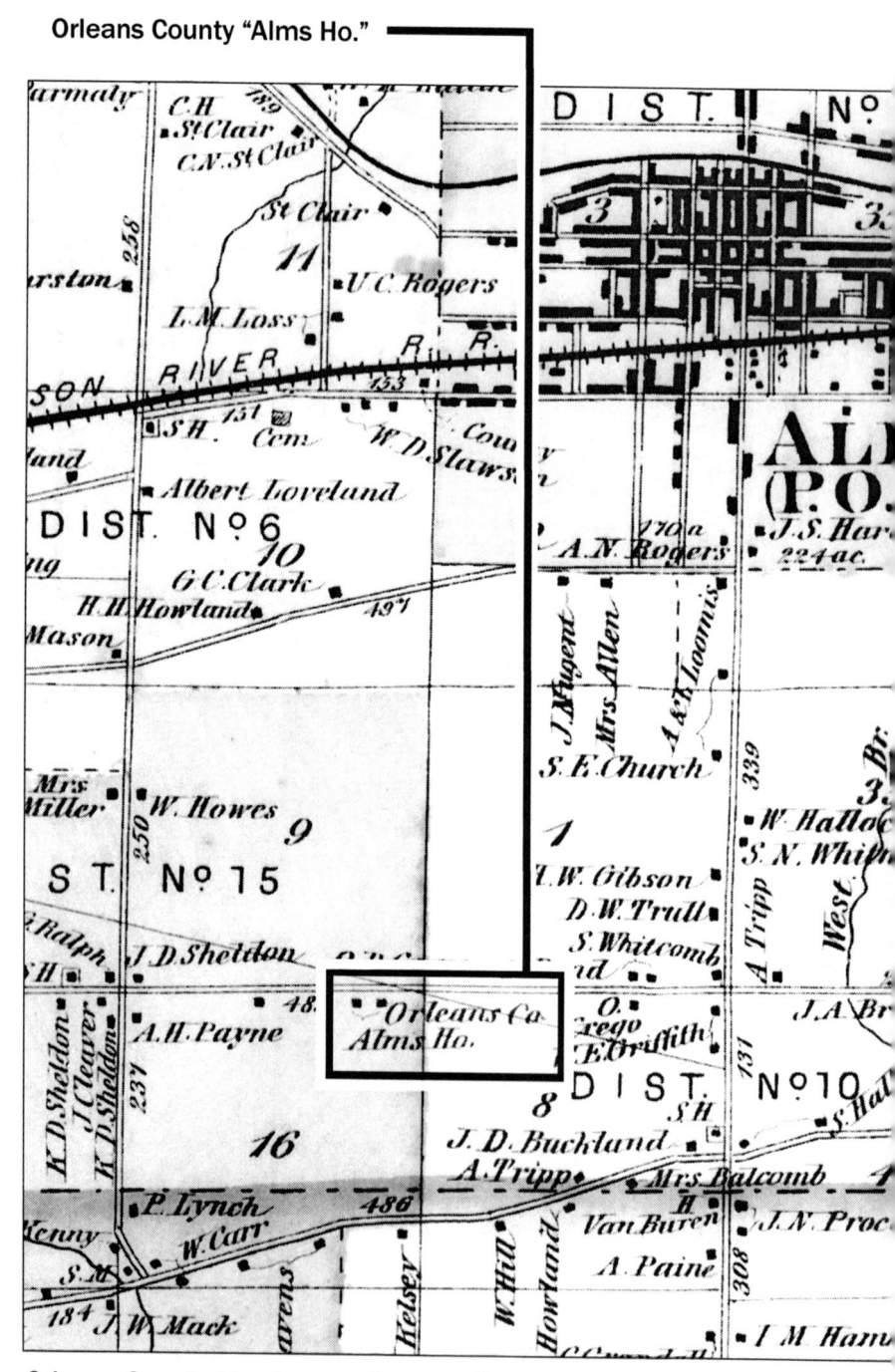

Orleans County Almshouse: "Orleans Co. Alms Ho.," 1875.

Map by D. G. Beers and Company

Ten years after the 1868 annual report, a new building was erected after the almshouse committee determined the old building was dilapidated and beyond repair.

In 1903, a county hospital was built fifty feet east of the new almshouse. The hospital buildings were used until 1960 when a new home for the "aged and infirm" was built west of Albion on Route 31.

As was the case with many of the county poorhouses, the Orleans County Home also served as a hospital not only for paupers and those incapable of caring for themselves but was also for the insane or "feebleminded." Individuals suffering from an injury, smallpox, chronic illness, or other diseases who were in need of care often occupied poorhouses while recuperating. The Orleans County Almshouse ledger dating from 1854 lists several entries noting that a person was provided shelter for a few days or weeks before they either recovered and left, "ran away," or found employment.

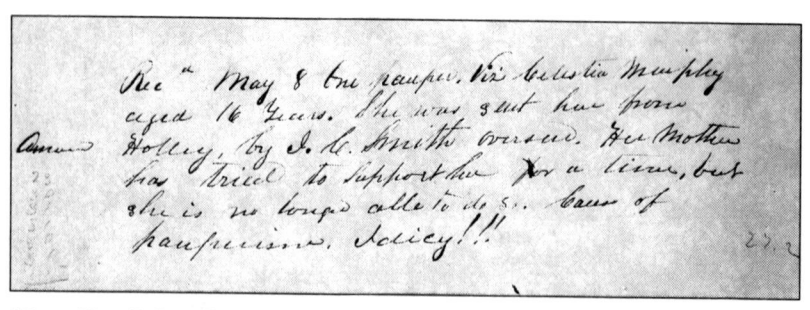

"Rec. May 8 One Pauper, Miss Celestia Murphy, aged 16 years. She was sent here from Holley, by I. C. Smith overseer. Her Mother has tried to support her for a time, but she is no longer able to do so. Cause of Pauperism. Idiocy!!!" Entry from the Orleans County Poorhouse Ledger.

Main building during winter at the new Orleans County Poorhouse building, late 1890s.

Driveway of the Orleans County Poorhouse, 1890s.

A report on the Orleans County Almshouse describes its living conditions and residents:

Yates Report, 1857 Investigation, from the "Annual Report of the State Board of Charities," New York:

> *This house is built of brick, forty by eighty feet, three stories high, connected with which is a farm of one hundred and seven acres, yielding an annual revenue of $721. The house is not ventilated. No provision for bathing except a shower bath...*
>
> *The number of inmates was forty: twenty males and twenty females, of whom sixteen were foreign and twenty-four native born, including eight children...As many as eight [paupers] are placed in a single room...The children of suitable age are sent to the district school. The supervisors have visited the house once this year.*
>
> *There have been five births and three deaths this past year. Of the inmates seven are lunatics; two male and five female, and all paupers...Three of the lunatics are confined in a hall opening into a yard; one is restrained by wearing mittens and one muffs. They are looked after by a pauper attendant, but receive no special medical attention. There are two idiots, both females; and one deaf and dumb.*
>
> *Four-fifths of the whole number come to want consequent upon habits of inebriation.*

Name, Benj. Davis Sex, Male Age, 32 Color, Black Civil State, Single Last Residence, _____
Record Number, 21 Birthplace (or County), Delaware How long in U. S.? 32 § How long in this State? _____
Date Admitted, Aug 15: a 1889 Has the person been naturalized? _____ If so, where and when? _____
Readmitted _____ 19 _____ If a widow,) was Husband a Citizen? _____ If an unmarried woman,) was Father a Citizen? _____
_____ 19 _____ Occupation, Labor Education, none Religion, Potatoes Habits, not good
_____ 19 _____ Physical Condition, Very Good Cause of Dependence, Feeble Minded, Epileptic
_____ 19 _____ Birthplace of Father (or Country,) Virginia Occupation, on Slavery Habits, _____
Birthplace of Mother (or Country,) _____ Condition of Parents, whether Dependent or Self
_____ Supporting, _____
_____ Is the person able to perform any Labor? Light work
Discharged _____ Has the person ever received Public Relief? _____ Where and when? _____
1894 Sept 8 19, 4 Has the person been an Inmate of an Almshouse or other Institution? _____
_____ 19 _____ Names and Addresses of Relatives or Friends, _____

                                                                    Jones of Albion

1894 entry from the Orleans County Almshouse ledger.

Infants at the Western House of Refuge. Photo: New York State Archives.

The Orleans County Home, which later also included a farm and a hospital, was destroyed—nothing remains of this facility.

Albion was also home to the Western House of Refuge, built in 1893, for "promiscuous and delinquent" adolescent females. Women with "criminal tendencies," a classification also encompassing "feeble-minded" women who, by their nature, were also thought to be promiscuous, were sent to the House of Refuge. Many girls from across the northern and western parts of the state were sent to Albion for reform. Today, the Albion Western House of Refuge exists as Albion Correctional Institution for Women.

"We have a burial ground that belonged to our old County Home (also known as "almshouse"). It is really not accessible to the public. It is now an abandoned field and wooded area [and] it is unknown exactly how many burials there are. Any record of that cemetery has been lost. I was able to put together a partial list of the burials there by going through the old town meeting books and getting what I could from the Alms House death report giving listings.

How they did the actual burials was rather sad. Each burial was given a cement marker about 6 inches square with a number chiseled into it. That number was the only identification of that person. As I said earlier, the burial book that showed which number belonged to which burial has been lost. So even if someone did find the old burial ground, all they would find was crumbling, numbered markers."

–From "The Poor House History by County" by Sharon A. Kerridge. Available online at http://www.poorhousestory.com/ORLEANS.htm.

Men's building at the Wyoming County Almshouse, early 1900s.

Photos courtesy of Doris Bannister, Wyoming County historian.

Wyoming County Poorhouse 1843-1959
Varysburg, New York

Wyoming County is among the smaller and less populated counties of Western New York, the last county to be formed when it separated from Genesee County in 1841. Noted for steep rolling hills, forests, rich farmland, and spectacular scenery, Wyoming County also features the magnificent Genesee River Gorge, the "Grand Canyon of the East," which runs along the county's eastern side and through Letchworth State Park. Even the largest communities are still small towns, and historically, agriculture played a primary role in the county's economy. The production of dairy products, vegetables, and maple syrup is still important to the county.

Located in Orangeville near the village of Varysburg, the Wyoming County Almshouse was situated among rolling hills and beautiful scenery. Rich farmland allowed the almshouse to be more self-sufficient, which influenced the decision to erect the building on the property.

Wyoming County Poorhouse: "County Poor House," 1866.

Map by Stone and Stewart

Views of Wyoming County Almshouse during the early 1900s. Men's building on left, keeper's quarters on right.

Back view of the men's building.

Residents of the Wyoming County Almshouse, Dick Wood (left) and John Morrisey (right), early 1900s.

View of Wyoming County Almshouse keeper's quarters during the early 1900s.

Front view of the keeper's quarters.

In 1843, the Wyoming County Home was finished and housed "47 paupers during its first year of operation, at a cost of 85 1/2¢ per person per week." Initially, those considered insane in Wyoming County were sent to Utica or the Genesee County Home and Insane Asylum. In 1864, the county erected a two-story building "to accommodate its own insane." Those living at the Genesee County Asylum in Bethany were transferred to the new building, which became known as the Wyoming County Lunatic Asylum.

As the county continued to purchase property at the site, more buildings were constructed. According to the *Historical Wyoming*, a publication produced by the Wyoming County Historical Society, "A so-called 'Idiot Asylum' was opened in 1874; a men's building in 1876 and a dining hall and women's building in 1878...." In later years, the entire facility was known as the Wyoming County Home.

One story often recounted about Wyoming County's almshouse is that of two little sisters. Abandoned by their parents in 1852 at about five and seven years of age, they were taken to the almshouse. The "idiotic" sister died shortly after being discovered along the road. The other sister, Sally, was said to be "deaf and dumb." When no one else would care for her, she remained a resident of the home for the remainder of her life. When she died in 1912, she was buried in the almshouse cemetery, "God's Acre."

In 1959, the Almshouse closed and its remaining parcels of land were sold to a local farmer. Eight men still residing at the almshouse at the time of its closure were transferred to the Genesee County Home in Bethany.

Today, the property and some of its remaining buildings continue to be used by the farmer who purchased it in 1960. The community also continues to use part of the county farm property as the 4-H camp called Camp Wyomoco. According to the *Historical Wyoming*, this camp helps youth to develop an interest in rural life "on the farm and in the home."

Bibliography

Bunis, Lois. "Notes: Talk Given to Chautauqua County Historical Society." Chautauqua County, New York.

Briggs, Jacqueline. *Erie County Home and Infirmary.* Unpublished manuscript.

Carleton, Will. "Over the Hill to the Poor House." *The Friendship Chronicle*, July, 28, 1880, Friendship, New York.

Census of Inmates in Almshouses and Poor Houses: 1875–1920. The New York State Archives, Albany, has almshouse records for all counties in New York.

Communications Collection. Niagara County Historian's Office, Lockport, New York.

Conklin, Susan L. *Genesee County Home (A Brief History).* Historian's note. Genesee County Historian's Office, Batavia, New York.

County Poor House and Farm. Niagara County (New York) Genealogical Society (located at Niagara County Historical Society Museum archives, Lockport, New York), 1897.

Crannell, Linda. "The Poorhouse Story," www.poorhousestory.com.

DeYounge, Bertha A. "Children at the Almshouse: How Little Ones Are Treated When in the County's Charge." *The Buffalo Courier*, 1800:6.

Disability History Museum. Straight Ahead Pictures, Inc., at www.disabilitymuseum.org.

"Erie County Almshouse and County Hospital." State University of New York at Buffalo, University Archives, Buffalo, New York.

"Erie County Poorhouse: Some Sharp Criticism of the Institution by the Hon. Wm. P. Letchworth." *Buffalo Daily Courier*, January 8, 1897.

Everts, L. H. *History of Cattaraugus Co., New York with Illustrations and Biographical Sketches of Some of its Prominent Men and Pioneers.* Philadelphia: J. B. Lippincott and Company, 1879.

Henry, Michelle. *Re-Dedication of the Cemetery for the Former County Poor Farm.* Dewittville, New York. Brochure for dedication ceremony, published by Chautauqua County Historian's Office, County Archives, Mayville, New York, 2001.

Higgins, Rosanne L. "The Biology of Poverty: Epidemiological Transition in Western New York." Dissertation, State University of New York at Buffalo, 1998.

Letchworth, William P. *A Record of Examinations and Official Inspections of Charitable Institutions*, State Board of Charities. Albany, New York, 1897. Viewed at Buffalo and Erie County Public Library, Buffalo, New York.

Letchworth, William P. *Reports on the Charities of the Eighth Judicial District of the State of New York.* Albany: 1878 and 1893. Report viewed at William Prior Letchworth Museum, Castile, New York.

Letchworth, William P. *Report on the Poorhouses in the Eighth Judicial District.* Albany: 1891 and 1896. Documents of the State of New York, Vol. 7.

Miller, Jeffrey. "Lime Lake: A Historical Review," from *Cattaraugus County: Southwestern New York State.* Published by Cattaraugus County Historical Museum and Research Center, Machias, New York, 2005.

Museum of disAbility History, Buffalo, New York. Also online at www.disabilitymuseum.org.

Newspaper Clippings Collection. Niagara County Historian's Office.

Orleans County Infirmary. Manuscript Collection. Orleans County Historian's Office, Albion, New York.

"Overview of Mental Health in New York and the Nation." New York State Archives, New York State Library, Albany, New York.

Parker, Bradley. "History of the Stone House," from *Cattaraugus County: Southwestern New York State*. Published by Cattaraugus County Historical Museum and Research Center, Machias, New York, 2005.

"Poorhouse History of Cattaraugus County," accessed at www.poorhousestory.com/CATTARAUGUS.htm.

Pratt, Weegie. "Plaque Marks First Schoolhouse." *LeRoy Pennysaver and News*, July 30, 2001, Leroy, New York.

Proceedings of the Superintendent of the Poor for Cattaraugus County. Albany: 1862. Cattaraugus County Historical Museum and Research Center, Machias, New York.

Pruyn, John V. L. *First Annual Report of the Board of State Commissioners of Public Charities*. Albany: 1868.

Report of Select Committee on Charitable Institutions, Poor Houses. Albany: The Argus Company, 1857.

Schneider, D. M. *The History of Public Welfare in New York State: 1609–1866*. Chicago: University of Chicago Press, 1938.

Smith, H. Perry., Ed. *History of the City of Buffalo and Erie County with Illustrations and Biographical Sketches of Some of its Prominent Men and Pioneers*. Vol. 1. Syracuse, NY: D. Mason and Co., 1884.

Spink, Mabel. "Orangeville, New York." *Historical Wyoming* 38.3. Wyoming County Historian's Office, Warsaw, New York, 1992.

Swedlund, Alan C., ed. *Human Biologists in the Archives: Demography, Health, Nutrition and Genetics in Historical Populations.* West Nyack, NY: Cambridge University Press, 2002.

The Centennial History of Chautauqua County. Vol. 1. Jamestown, NY: The Chautauqua History Company, 1904.

Towne, Ezra T. *Social Problems: A Study of Present-Day Social Conditions.* New York: The Macmillan Company, 1927.

Venema, Janny. *Beverwijck: A Dutch Village on the American Frontier, 1652–1664.* Albany: SUNY Press, 2003.

82   On the Edge of Town: *Almshouses of Western New York*

Acknowledgments

The Museum of disABILITY History and People Inc. wish to thank the following county historians and citizens for their invaluable contributions of time, resources, and rare photographs that made this publication possible.

Allegany County:
Craig Braack, county historian

Cattaraugus County:
Bradley Parker, Trustee, Cattaraugus County Historical Society
Carol Ruth, county historian
Sharon Fellows, Cattaraugus County Historical Research Museum and Research Center, Machias, New York.

Chautauqua County:
Jack Ericson, photographs from his private collection
Michelle Henry, county historian

Erie County:
Jacqueline Briggs, retired medical records archivist for the Erie County Home and Infirmary

Edward Leisner, W. Yerby Jones Memorial Library, Erie County Medical Center

Linda Lohr, manager, History of Medicine Collection, State University of New York at Buffalo

William H. Seiner, director, Buffalo and Erie County Historical Society

Patricia Virgil, director, Buffalo and Erie County Historical Society Library and Archives

Genesee County:
Lori Carlson, Rolling Hills Country Mall
Susan L. Conklin, county historian
Irene Walter, LeRoy town historian

Niagara County:
Melissa Dunlap, director, Niagara County Historical Society, Lockport, New York
Ann Marie Linnaberry, Niagara County Historical Society
Marcia Rivers, deputy county historian (2006)
Catherine L. Emerson, Craig E. Bacon, Ronald F. Cary, Niagara County Historian's Office, Lockport, New York (2010)

Orleans County:
C. W. Lattin, county historian

Wyoming County:
Doris Bannister, county historian
William Prior Letchworth Museum, Castile, New York

The Museum of disABILITY History staff also wishes to thank Melissa Royer for her patient editing skills, Ray Graf and Marlena Heintz for their assistance with this publication, and Paul Cheteny for his additional research on poorhouses. We also thank People Inc. executives James M. Boles, EdD, president and CEO, and Francisco M. Vasquez, PhD, executive vice president, for their support of this project.

Index

A
Allegany County Home 7

B
Bacon, Craig E. 84
Bannister, Doris 68, 84
Braack, Craig 6
Briggs, Jacqueline 77, 83
Bunis, Lois 77

C
Carleton, Will 77
Carlson, Lori 84
Cary, Ronald F. 84
Cattaraugus County Almshouse 7
Census of Inmates in Almshouses and Poor Houses 77
Chautauqua County Home 7
Conklin, Susan L. 38, 77, 84
Crannell, Linda 78

D
DeYounge, Bertha A. 78
Dix, Dorothea 3
Dunlap, Melissa 84

E
Emerson, Catherine L. 84
Ericson, Jack 20, 83
Erie County Home and Infirmary 37
Erie County Poorhouse 7
Everts, L. H. 78

F
Fellows, Sharon 83

G
Genesee County Home 7

H
Henry, Michelle 78, 83

Higgins, Rosanne L. 79
Home for the Friendless 51, 52

I
Indoor Relief 2

K
Kerridge, Sharon A. 67

L
Lattin, C. W. 56, 84
Leisner, Edward 84
Letchworth, William P. 79
Linnaberry, Ann Marie 84
Lohr, Linda 84

M
Miller, Jeffrey 79
Morrisey, John 73

N
Niagara County Almshouse 7
Niagara County Infirmary 53
Niagara County Poorhouse 51

O
Oppenheim, James 1
Orleans County Almshouse 7
Outdoor Relief 2

P
Parker, Bradley 80, 83
Pratt, Weegie 80
Pruyn, John V. L. 80

R
Rivers, Marcia 84
Ruth, Carol 12, 83

S
Schneider, D. M. 80
Seiner, William H. 84
Smith, H. Perry 80
Spink, Mabel 81
State Asylum for Idiots 3
Swedlund, Alan C. 81

T
Towne, Ezra T. 81

V
Venema, Janny 81
Virgil, Patricia 84

W
Walter, Irene 84
Western House of Refuge 66
Wood, Dick 73
Wyndham Lawn Home for Children 51
Wyoming County Poorhouse 7

Y
Yates Report 64

CPSIA information can be obtained at www.ICGtesting.com
Printed in the USA
LVOW06s1200100214

373057LV00001B/145/P